Tree Falling in Forest

Poems

Guntis Brazma

ISMN: 9798684533792

I would like to express appreciation to Tony Newton for including poems
included in this collection: *Darkest Corner of Heart, Prisoner, My Demons,
The Holy Word* and *Vine from My Skull* in *Deathly Sorrow: A collection of
Dark Poetry.*

Warning!
May contain sugar and acid

Contents

Heart on Your Plate

Here is my heart
On your plate

Carefully selected
And marinated
In different experiences

It's been cooked
In your beauty
Sorry if it's overcooked
It may be a little too soft

Rested in loneliness
Decorated
With poems and stories
And covered
With spicy sense of humour

Now take a bite
And tell me what you think

Silent Cry

I told you so much when I was alone
But when I saw you I vanished like stone
From the surface of water deep as a well
Only thin layer divides it from hell

Leaves growing brown no matter what season
Stars falling down for a cause and a reason
It's cold and it's wet there is a creepy sensation
Death isn't a threat it's a temptation

I told you it all from underneath of the grass
Behind a brick wall through a bulletproof glass
I told you before from out of your sight
I never could reach your glorious height

A Tribute to Beauty

I know
You're not saving the World
I know
You are not trying to keep
The snow
Is melting in sun rays
And now
You are hidden so deep

The bless
Of the beautiful view
The mess
Of discovering new
The less
Of distracting reviews
The rest
Are drowning in you

So still

Like a marble statute

Is guilt

Of stealing the cute

I will

Defend and refute

The bill

Of searching for you

The Peace of Thunder

Gloomy prediction darkens frying skies
You know this heat was gonna have to end
The land is thirsty and it's full of flies
It's been too much and so the storm is sent

Wind comes like prophet to prepare the way
Sweeps all the dust and levels highest dunes
Then all the doubts he takes and blows away
While chimneys plays prelude in eerie tune

Drop of the certainty of what is up to happen
Baptizes soil and makes its way to roots
And then it comes without a grace or passion
It makes you feel your outfit and your boots

The air around is bubbling and fizzy
No one is there they're hiding from the rain
Even puddles on the street are getting busy
They rushes to be first at closest drain

Then sudden light fills every gap and corner
A tree gets split with great and shiny sword
And it keeps sparking and it goes on burning
As it now rests on heavy voltage cords

A mighty voice although it sounds so angry

It seem to me pronouncing word of peace

At least you know that everything has happened

And so at least you are able now to breathe

Leave Me

Leave me

In this rotting reality

I'm alright with it

Since I know

That you know

That I loved you so

The Leaf

She leaves the branch

And starts to dance

As wind takes her under his arm

She's feeling so free

Away from that tree

And taken by music and charm

She's sexy she's brilliant

She dance like Brazilian

She takes all the party ahead

The plastic and wood

Umbrella and hood

And even the roof of the shed

She's dancing so high

She's dancing so low

There is no more need to pretend

She runs down the street

Gets stuck with her feet

In a puddle of water

The end

Don't Sing this Song

Don't sing this song can't take it any more
I know the lyrics and I know the chords
And I have heard this melody before
It is about the same unspoken words

Don't pick again the dirty bits and dust
The purulence of rotten parts of heart
I know I have to do I know I must
I just don't know from where to have a start

Don't rip the scab just leave it where it is
It took some time for it to dry and form
I do not want such deep analysis
I better live as if it was a norm

Don't try to change it never has been done
I do not know what I've been living for
There is no lesson and there is no fun
So please don't sing this ballad any more

I Don't Talk to the Wind

I never talk to the wind
Its breath is too deep for my hand
Its tears are too many to sing
Its all too much to understand

I take some of it in my breath
Not much only a little bit
I'm afraid that anything more
Can make me a part of it

And then I would fly below stars
Maybe make friends with a few
I would forget all my scars
But I'd be too far above you

...geddon

NASA is warning
World's going to end
If you've got some money
It's last chance to spend
A gigantic rock piece
Is coming for us
To show us some magic
And turn into dust

I'm eating my sandwich
Sky's turning red
It's surely the last time
I bite into bread
Whatever comes after
It's over right now
I'd like to survive but
Hell I don't know how

It finally hits then
Our planet in face
The nature is showing
Its greatest disgrace
Everything's burning
From buildings to grass
If you survived shock wave
You'll be poisoned by gas

Crack in the Ceiling

I lie on my bed
And just stare in the ceiling
There is a crack

Like a tree
Growing
Spreading his branches

Like a stick man
Having a laugh
Raised his hands in a joy

Like a gap
Between the inner
And the outer me

Like a pointless battle
Between caffeine
And exhaustion

My eyes are itching
It may be tiredness
It may be dust falling from the crack

I'd better close my eyes
I've been looking at it
For too long

I know the crack is still there
Like a reminder
Like a depressing mandala

Little scary void
Between two plains of matter
Separating

It looks at me
From above
That stick man or that tree

And maybe sees
A crack
In the middle of the bed

My Demons

The night is getting rid of the sun
Lonely cloud is chasing the stars
Day is fading like smoke from a gun
And some cat is licking his scars

Owls start summoning demons
You don't need to call them twice
Not sure I'm awake or I'm dreaming
But I know that my soul is the price

Here comes the demon of sadness
Keeping me tied to the quilt
And then to deepen my madness
His brother the spirit of guilt

And out of the darkened corners
Lurking at me with a spear
Adding his part to this welter
His majesty spirit of fear

And then the worthlessness demon
Oh didn't notice he's here
And he says for you little moron
The end of the world is near

And they start eating my soul
Getting high like from opium
But then I stand up on my feet
I say guys how about rum

They freeze for a moment and listen
And they stop doing their rife
Soon we are drunk and singing
And taking a piss out of life

So I made friends with my demons
I'm not afraid them at all
Just hope that next time they come
They'll bring their own alcohol

Painting

Without a particular meaning
Just vision without any frame
Guided by colours and feeling
The paintbrush is starting its game

Confused in the desert of canvas
Afraid to make a wrong move
The brush barely touches the surface
In doubt and self-disapproved

It walks in the footprints of pencil
Though pencil hasn't done much
But the trail shines in its freshness
Encouraging every new touch

Soon the paintbrush has hovered
Every place and spot that is known
And all the footprints are covered
Leaving it free but alone

Now light is falling so tense
And paint is dripping like sweat
It gains some experience
But the image is not perfect yet

When the hope seem to be lacking
That the god of beauty is pleased
The dam of hardness start cracking
And sense of reward is released

The shapes and the shadows unfold
And picture start looking well
The story is now to be told
It's sealed like a pearl in a shell

Distant Train

A train full with people
Their goals to reach
They're passing the steeples
They're passing the beach

I don't know who are they
They don't know I'm here
Maybe they're happy
But they could be in tears

I smile to myself
And I give it a wink
I wish I was more to you
But I wish many things

It is what it is
It's not coming close
It's a train in a distance
It goes where it goes

Eagle

I am the first to see the rising sun
And last to say goodbye to ditching day
I'm born and raised below the clear heavens
And through them also goes my lonely ways

It is my home the forest and the fountain
Where I've been pushed from edge until I fly
And fought the winds there side by side with mountains
Above the tree tops where no one hears you cry

Some might be envy but there is no reason
You see that not in vain I have this beak
I'm not enjoying view it's hunting season
And I don't recommend to play the hide and seek

My wings are tired measuring the land
I always hunt sometimes it feels so boring
Sometimes I wish I had a pair of hands
To make some pancakes in a Sunday morning

I have a nest I must provide with yield
I look and catch this is my only habit
Look there is rat it runs across the field
I'll take it home my kids are gonna love it

Do You Touch

Do you touch my heart
When it's about to fall
I know you are inside
Do you touch the wall

Do you touch the storm
That I'm going through
Apart from lack of smile
I keep away from you

Do you touch my pain
Is it in my eyes
Or it's down the drain
With love and other lies

Do you touch the feeling
That I try to preach
Do you touch my person
Do you even reach

Frozen

Sizzling snowflakes
Covers the track
A pair of footprints
Behind your back

Once flowing river
And bushes of clover
Don't even shiver
As you walk over

Puddle on pavement
Frozen and neat
Crunches like promise
Under your feet

Day mixed with night
Whatever you flatter
It's dark or it's bright
It no longer matters

Foot on the Way

A clear and cold water spring
For a hot summer day
Could be a refreshing drink
You put your foot in it's way

It tried to get then around
To flow still if it may
Could later become a river
You put your foot in it's way

Soaked back into the ground
To later emerge as a lake
Could be still like a mirror
You put your foot in it's way

It came as boiling hot source
For some kind of beauty to stay
Could be a wild natural sauna
You put your foot in it's way

It was too late to say no
A cloud raised black and grey
It erupted as a volcano
No foot could be in it's way

Well we're going through stages

It just needed to let it out

Now it'll be calm for ages

Yeah but the village is burned

Firewood

A spark from out of nowhere
Lit up the dark around
I start to feel alive
On this open ground

Still shy and little flames
So innocent and fresh
Start climbing up my body
Dry veiny wooden flesh

Then flames are going higher
They try to reach the moon
Please come and burn with me
Or it will end too soon

Collapsed within myself
So empty I'm inside
And all that's left of me
Is nothing to abide

I calm and my reflection
Is dying in your lashes
My heart gets slowly coated
In flapping flakes of ashes

Blue dying lonely flames
Comes ever less and lower
Just to make you think
The party isn't over

Distance

I walked the street
Minding my shopping
And I think I saw you
From a distance

I am not sure
That it was you
I couldn't really see
From a distance

You crossed the road
You arranged your hood
And probably saw me
From a distance

When you were done
You tried to wave me
But hesitated
From a distance

That's what it looked like
I am not sure
I'm still deciding
From a distance

Night

It's night
The world is sleepy
It's dark
But not completely

The sun
Is just somewhere else
I try
To assemble myself

Don't know
I can't really see
If you
Are here or you flee

What if
That flash and that spark
Were you
With me in the dark

Explosion

Chaos in my head
Hundreds of thoughts
Thousands
Of thoughts about them

Strategies
Riddles
Problems
Solutions

Probabilities
Possibilities
Capabilities
Abilities

Attractions
Distractions
Fractions

This is how
Dynamite works

Killing a Dream

I have a dream
Lord I can't fill
I have to live with it
Or to kill

But you can't kill a dream
Can you

Dream will tear you apart
Dying
But you still catch yourself
Trying

Because you can't kill a dream
Can you

I Heard a Sound

I heard a sound
And I don't know what it was
It didn't sound like anything
Significant

So I didn't go to see
Where the sound was from
I just carried on with my own things

As the time went
The sound settled in my mind
It got louder and louder there

As it became disturbing
I started to build theories
On what it was

The position of insignificance
Became my defence strategy
Against these theories

Defence was weak though
It barely survived
The guilt and worries
About not finding the source
Of the sound

The sound is amplifying itself
The source is long gone
Here I am

This Door

If I came in through this door
While I'm writing this poem
How would I welcome me

Would I even thank me for coming
Would I poke me with guilt
Or encourage for more success

Would I make a cup of tee
If I was thirsty
Or I would give me chores instead

Would I sit and tell about the issues
Or I would listen to my needs
Or we would just exchange excuses

Would I thank me
That would feel weird
That doesn't happen often

I often come through this door
But have I paid enough attention
To how do I make me feel

Onlineliness

The dots are jumping
Someone's typing
They disappear
And jump again

As long as they jump
I'm fed with illusion
Of conversation

And two minutes later
The message
Is composed

Hi sorry I'm busy now
Seen

That's fine
See you another time
Seen

Void

I wonder
If they're emptier
Who doesn't have
The void inside
That burns to get filled

I wonder
If that everyday
Dreamless fullfillness
Isn't just a form
Of emptiness

I wonder
If Buddha when he emptied his mind
Wanted to free the space
Or to gain the void
To fuel
His ever inexplicable quest

Storm of Love

You are not always that ready
For what you are going to do
Days carry pretty much steady
Your peaceful boat of life through

But peace is absence of chaos
Not saying it's always the same
Not always with promise to save us
It can be a storm taking aim

When it approaches you flowing
Your eyes are looking away
So tempting inviting and glowing
That you are loosing your way

You fight with waves you're creating
You fall out of boat without wind
You are risking of suffocating
While thinking you're having the wings

Then losing your conscious awareness
You think you are reaching the skies
If lucky then unarmed and helpless
You open another two eyes

Why to Love

Why to burn
In sweetness of the pain
Why to wait
And freeze in snow and rain

Why to fall
And sacrifice your dreams
Why to find
That nothing's what it seems

Why to steal
A heart from other house
Why to be
A captive of a spouse

Why to dance
At music you don't know
Why to look
For treasure down below

Why to give
The light to other lives
Why to stuck
At work just to provide

Why to hope

Tomorrow be the same

When you know

That heart was never tamed

Word Games

We're playing our game with the words
I throw them on table like dice
But words can have different meaning
If you play with them clever and nice

And if you are trying to catch me
You are catching a wind of a kind
Because there are so many words
I can easily hide behind

I cautiously looked around
Words were all over the place
What if behind some of them
I found your beautiful face

Then once you almost found me
I pulled over joke as a sheet
That joke was as cold as ice
Though I was there dying from heat

But time it flies like a rocket
It never leaves things the same
My tongue now stays in my pocket
Till next time we'll play our game

Prisoner

Muffled echoes from every step of guards
In the corridors is only source of time
Behind the doors of welded iron bars
Appears a bowl in it some kind of slime

It will be fine for ever starving body
I am so grateful for everything I get
I have become a life denying zombie
Who long has died but not accepted yet

Rats are coming eating from my hand
When visiting me here once in a while
Skulls in the corner they'll never see their land
Gives every day a reassuring smile

But what would happen if in a summer day
A guard would say your serving time is done
And I would have to leave and go away
In choking freshness and the blinding sun

I'd kill somebody in the night at tavern
To get back here I wouldn't be that strong
I'm not just prisoner of that whoever governs
I'm also prisoner of being here so long

Photography

Stay still this is the correct angle
And when I give the sign to smile say cheese
The truest you is ready to untangle
When button clicks and diaphragm sneeze

And light that broke against your face
Enters the aperture to settle on a frame
I'm glad it found its mission and its place
To be a proof that you are still the same

Your body is a land your eyes are portal
To summon you inspect and magnify
This is the price when you become immortal
A moment that's arrested on the fly

No final touch to add some special look
Like when you make a painting or you write
Now it will stay exactly as I took
And fixed it all in shades of black and white

It's not just image on a glossy paper
You contribute the Universe your dime
It is your ticket to be now and later
At first companion then witness of the time

And thank you I'm grateful for your duty

And your existence able to unfold

To let create this artefact of beauty

A pocket version of your precious soul

Radio Man

There was a man

He worked for radio

From early morning

To late night

He informed

Entertained

And educated

He warned

And he encouraged

For everyone in the town

He was a part of life

But one day he left

Some listeners asked

Why did you leave your job

But most of them

Didn't

Silence

Have your silence
I still can't decide
Is it what you want
Or need

You're gonna go for more
Anyway
And I'll have more
For me

I feel a bit guilty
Enjoying it
How about you

Don't answer
Have your silence
Have a good silence

Darkest Corner of Heart

God when I see the ugly things and beauty
You put me in to see if I can deal
It doesn't work the way you have designed me
Sometimes I even wish I couldn't feel

Then all the colours that everyday surrounds me
They start to pale and look like but a waste
I live my days without a real feeling
I eat my food it doesn't have its taste

And then I fill my empty days with dreaming
Life passes by so silent like a dart
Lord can you hear my prayer that is streaming
From darkest corner of my broken heart

I'll take a cup with all my hidden wishes
I know it can be poison if I drink
With shaken hands I lift it to my lips
For every thought I can't afford to think

Diamond

I had a diamond for you
It was rare big and polished
With exceptional care

I gave it to you
But your bag was already full
With cobbles and seashells

You put the diamond on top
It fell and shattered
Against the floor

You picked up
An insignificant piece
With no shape

And you said
Beautiful

A Man with a Clock on His Face

I saw a man
With a clock on his face
The clock was stuck
Somewhere around late evening

It would work
It would show the time
But its hands were tied

What do you want
I asked the man
Why there is no movement
On your face
As if it was stuck
Somewhere around late evening

Do you want a clock
That goes on without a spring
Or a spring that goes on without a clock

Spring without a clock

Never gets satisfied

In summer

And never gives fruits

Never faces the clock

Why can't you face the clock

I can't fall asleep

The man said

To slip into the darkness

Letting the weakness

Govern my body

And then wake up

Knowing

That my hands are still tied

Question

If you have to go now
Where there is no return
Did you believe in God

I'm asking you just in case
I want to go to the same place

Vine from My Skull

Did you drink vine from my skull
I was dizzy for no apparent reason
Your lips were so red your eyes so full
You must've been up to some treason

It did feel like my fermented soul
Was rinsing through teeth and your tongue
I am long ago dead as a whole
You'll always and forever be young

You swallowed my pleasure and joy
It dropped down to soak in your blood
You held then my skull like a toy
I hope you don't leave it in mud

My soul then it ran through your body
And sank into your mind like a well
To visit your most violent wishes
That will lead us both to the hell

Smoke in My Head

A cloud of light and ashes
So light and fluid thread
Surrounding all it clashes
That's smoke in my own head

I try to stop it sometimes
And put a trap ahead
It flows between my fingers
That smoke in my own head

And every little blowing
Of words that someone said
Makes swirling without slowing
The smoke in my own head

It dances and it changes
It never goes to bed
The demons and the angels
Just smoke in my own head

There must be questions burning
With a flame heartbroken red
I can't see through the smoke
The smoke in my own head

And all I know is real
My water and my bread
My truth as hard as steel
Just smoke in my own head

But when it clears at times
I see where I've been led
I've tried to find what rhymes
With smoke in my own head

Traitor

I'm sorry brother for this bloody blade
Leaving you unable for a question
It is one tree from which we both are made
But branches grew in opposite directions

I know that feeling when the sharpest cutter
Gets to the vessel of what you love in life
And cuts it softly softly like a butter
Touched by rage and fire heated knife

You must accept I know that it's uneasy
But it would blow just anybody's mind
The chance that life has offered me so cheesy
To better off by only being blind

And I must take it for it seldom happens
When in your eyes the satisfaction screams
To become from sailor to the captain
Or to swim up from the whey to very cream

There is a price I'm paying for this glory
I'm sometimes losing all my sleep in bed
That's why I want to come and say I'm sorry
To silence all these voices in my head

Now that we have this embarrassing collision

And you must take from me this deadly slam

You probably would make the same decision

But you are not as gifted as I am

Loneliness

It's dark outside and it has darkened blue
Just checking on my online ghosts tonight
Oh loneliness it's you again how are you
I didn't know that you'll be in my sight

You come across these days so very often
Your smile is pale and dress is blurry grey
Sit down I'll get some tea and take a muffin
We can then chat I've got some things to say

So how you've been how many have you seen
I guess a lot you're popular these days
Remember though that you are just a guest
Don't stay too long and sooner go away

And when I'm having time with other people
Don't follow me so close that they can see
You try to steal me like some kind of burgle
I want you try to leave my self to me

Now I don't mind to see you now and then
When darkness lights the candles on the street
Just don't be jealous it is silly when
I have sometimes somebody else to meet

No wait I didn't mean to hurt you

Don't have to leave me sipping tea right now

Your dress just waves that spider tailored for you

As now you run like arrow from the bow

Clouds

I remember when I was a boy
And didn't need money for rent
Apart from some broken toys
Didn't know what broken meant

I laid on a blanket outside
The sun was rubbing my belly
Stuffed with potatoes and meatballs
And I watched clouds like a telly

They passed by my eyes and swirled
Changing into different things
Opening another new world
With its own joy and suffering

Two clouds came close together
Right above top of that tree
And another came out a lot smaller
It looked like a chicken to me

Many gathered like crowds
That was a good view to see
They looked like a kind of orchestra
Playing some nice symphony

Two others they melted in one
And they formed shape of a heart
The third ran through like an arrow
Then split the two sides apart

One of them looked like a pillow
I wanted to get there and hide
But a worker with shiny pickaxe
Was mining its golden side

One cloud was limping across
Like an old man with a stick
Tried to keep up with others
But he was no longer that quick

Some of them looked like people
Enjoying this beautiful day
A bird crossed the skies maybe eagle
Then angels danced them away

Ah those days of my childhood
Didn't look into things very deep
Don't know what happened to chicken
I guess I was falling in sleep

Open the Window

Open the window
The air is stuck and is not able to move
It sits on your chest
Like a hidden shame
Like a given up initiative
Like a question left burning
In an ash tray

Open the window
Let the tree in
And the birds with their chaotic song
And the fresh sun rays
That has broke through the clouds
And are queuing
At your closed window

Open the window
For the greenness of the plants
And the redness of the sky
The silence of the wind
And the peace of the rain

Open the window
Stop pretending
That you can afford to be poor

Hourglass

You know
How hourglass works

You give up everything
And wait
While time fills you
Again

Through a little opening
Where the past
And the future
Meets

Sometimes
It seems enough
Sometimes
It seems too much

Sometimes
You can't give up
Because the hourglass
Is broken
And the sand
Never stops pouring

Stop Burning Me

Stop burning me with beauty
My skin is turning black
My soul is leaving body
And I can not hold it back

My brain is drying quickly
It needs some drop of hope
Not sure if it's still working
I don't know how to cope

There is no shadow from you
You follow in my mind
You make my head exhausted
Your beauty makes me blind

Stop burning me with beauty
It is no longer fun
I feel like fried potato
A vampire in the sun

Kill Me

She asked him sweetly
Do you enjoy your wine
He humbly replied
With you
I would enjoy poison

He knew what he said
He had been drinking that poison
Ever since their glances met

He was already dying
When he said kill me
Kill me now

They killed their minds
And dumped their bodies
In each other's
Heartbeats

Survivor

It's not the end as you have tried to prove me
And made me to accept the guilt and shame
And bend so low like I was fruitful pear tree
But this is sure I am no more the same

I gave up all my treasure and my pride
I emptied for you all my fulfilled barn
But you forgot that taking up this side
I also reasoned and I also learned

You saw me crawling as if I was a beggar
Enjoying me at level of a spit
Now you have spent and wasted all your luck
While I was picking all the crumbs of it

And now we are at point where we are equal
This thing is finally somehow getting done
We're meeting there like vulture and an eagle
We both have single bullet in the gun

Wave

Every other wave
Is higher than the last
Expectations drops
But hopes are rising fast

Every other wave
Is stronger than we've seen
As you struggle staying
Anywhere between

Every other wave
Is closer to the coast
You are always slave
Of what you fancy most

Every other wave
Brings you again to top
Of promise that you made
To never dare to stop

Spider

Now that you are in better hands
Let me take care of your needs
I know they all have let you down
With their selfishness and their greed

It's quiet I don't like when it's noisy
Outside they roar like a storm
Let me just wrap you nice and cosy
You will be tranquil and warm

You see I never attack anyone
I just take care of my guests
All the way here before you're done
I will follow any requests

You don't have to be lonely here
You can invite your friends
Friendship shall not disappear
And love - love never ends

You can share your life with them
And yes indeed your death
It would be like a social network
Connected before your last breath

The power of connectivity
Is quite underestimated
If you will start to wiggle and twist
So will all those connected

Wiggle wiggle wiggle

Oh the sun is now going down
I think it would be just right
If I crawled now to my new friend
And quietly kissed goodnight

Free Fall

I don't want to hold on
I want to fall
To fall in sleep
To fall in sin
To fall in love
Wherever
In a free fall

I don't want to think good
And neither bad
I want to let it all go
In a free fall

You call me crazy
You call me insane
But if you look at your life
It's also a free fall

How Much You Love

You almost did the task
But got a stain on glove
And now they come and ask
How much you really love

Besides your best of effort
And what you have become
You didn't write a letter
How much you really love

Day followed by a day
You fly through like a dove
But still avoid to say
How much you really love

It almost leaves your mind
And disappears above
But something still reminds
How much you really love

Fool

Groups of artists one by one performing
Some losers goes to guillotine outside
King feels that now he wants some joking
Let's see the fools performance and his pride

Among spectators there is also princess
She smiles at me encouraging and meek
Her hair is gold and eyes are made of crystals
And warmest sun rays are resting on her cheek

Then everything around me disappears
Like I was under numbing mindless spell
And I forget it all yes even fears
And even program that I came to sell

Then all I see upon this sudden darkness
Is princess and her body and her lips
Guests voices mutes in unimportant starkness
And tingles in my baffled fingertips

And I just say first thing that's in my head
I do not care that later I get slaughtered
I look into the eyes of king instead
I want to ask the hand of your own daughter

Kings laughter can be heard beyond the borders
He laughs so hard he almost drops his crown
And people seem be taking this as order
As they laugh too till king himself calms down

It feels like they are laughing half a day
Some shaking like a sick and dying cow
But princess leaves she cries and goes away
She feels she has become a joke somehow

Oh how I hate them I wish they all be dying
I wish they all turned into gnome or elf
But even more I want to go outside
Outside the castle and guillotine my self

But king then says this fool is awesome
You must be best of artists in their pool
I fake a smile I straighten up my body
It's joker majesty it's joker not a fool

Caller

We've split the floods in heavy rain
And we have slipped on snow and ice
But you decided then again
Another time to roll the dice

You picked the phone you had a call
I guess it was your shooting star
As we were passing city walls
And then you asked to stop the car

I still don't know who was the caller
And yet it's taking us apart
I just watch as you look smaller
In the mirror of my car

Coin for Luck

I'm shaken by the winds of change
My life gets redefined
My broken branches rearrange
In the river of the time

They fall like memories in stream
That carries them away
My intentions and my dreams
My dark and brighter days

I stop on bridge and I look down
Not all of it is gone
Some memories refuse to drown
As I just carry on

I see them still even today
They're jammed and they are stuck
I dropped a coin and walked away
I dropped that coin for luck

The Holy Word

In the beginning there was a Word
And it spread between the folks
Then it was given wealth and sword
To punish any who provokes

The story goes you know it all
From virgin birth to shameful cross
But even strongest cities fall
And all the glory can be lost

I loved You dearly all was fine
You gave me comfort of a sort
But once You really crossed the line
When You ran one angel short

It was not to comprehend
I asked my questions clear and sound
I saw there really is no end
If skies don't end above the clouds

I saw the beauty of the space
And the smallness of my self
I'm sorry You were then replaced
And left collecting dust in shelf

I sometimes miss that sense of care

Ever since I've cut the chord

Jesus said may peace be with you

I say rest in peace my Lord

Carnival

The music stirs up the room
And turns the guests into blizzard
They spiral around the fumes
The notes and the rhythm they've heard

Witches and devils start dancing
And princes and angels alike
You cannot just stay there balancing
At the face of this magical strike

Everyone's acting their role
Movements are matching their suits
They all have their own secret goals
They have come here to pursuit

And masks they cover their nose
You still see their lips and their glance
They pretend not knowing each other
For this one intimate dance

Soon though they turn into humans
From bears owls and elves
Acted and real amusement
Takes place at the hour of twelve

The carnival still continues

Although the guests are gone

It's just that their masks are removed

The masks that has never been on

Echoes

Give up
Up up up

There is no hope
Hope hope hope

There is no future
Future future future

Is anything there
Her her her

In the Rain

When the clouds are stealing light
And the darkness fills the scene
And the famous silver side
Is nowhere to be seen

You look through crying window
With your lovely longing eyes
Aching for some sunlight
From the dark and busy skies

You are not in there alone
Don't feel it as a pain
For none of us is gone
It's me here in the rain

Dandelion

In a meadow next to forest
All kinds of flowers bloom
Insignificant like the truth
There is a dandelion too
Like the truth

Been there and always will be
It will die and then reload
It can emerge through concrete
In the middle of the road
Like the truth

It's beautiful it's ugly
It doesn't make a sound
But when it's finished blooming
Even kids blows it around
Like the truth

You like them next to pavement
You may blow away it's seeds
But in your well groomed garden
They are nothing but some weeds
Like the truth

So strong but they are bleeding

When torn away from land

I remember from my childhood

White blood that sticks to hands

Like the truth

In a meadow next to forest

All kinds of flowers bloom

Insignificant like the truth

There is a dandelion too

Like the truth

Event Horizon

I saw you from a distance
Wrapped in cosmic light
Since then my whole existence
Became your satellite

Through deserts of the darkness
The nebulas of doubt
The gravity of kindness
Start pulling me about

And then before you know it
We are so close but then
I run within my orbit
So far away again

But as we learn each other
The orbit starts get smaller
The speed and mass increases
The pull feels even stronger

Your beauty bends the space
And everything I could
I'd do it for a place
Within your arms for good

Night Whisper

Hey are you now awake
I just saw you in my dream
I was in some kind of trouble
And you were there to help me

You said me so beautiful words
Just to make me feel better
You comforted me and encouraged
As I snuggled to your soft sweater

Hey I am sorry to bother
But I wanted to ask to you
That dream was so realistic
Did you just see that dream too

Old Travellers Bag

I want to buy a travellers bag
Old bag that's been used
Ever since I wanted
To live a wanderer's life

I don't need it big
Just for essentials
To hold my shoes
When I want to go bare
Or a sip for the road
Or a song
About crossing horizon

I want an old bag
That's already seen
Both sides of the road
And the shortcuts
Through the thorns
And has been hanging
On a strong hand
Above wild waters

I want to buy an old

Travellers bag

I have tried every

Shop and store

They all sell only

New bags

Water

It can be hot it can be cold
It can be cool it can be warm
Water is always ready
To be the way
You are comfortable with it

Open the tap
Look up
And let it flow through your hair

It fills your hair with calmness
It makes them submissive
It relaxes them
While gently stroking your scalp

Then it slides down to your neck
Enjoying the ride
To your shoulder
To your chest

Water is alive

But it has no shape

So it takes yours

By being so much close

To what you are

To what you are like

To what you like

It slides by your beauty

And your imperfections

Your pride and your shame

And even if the difference is arguable

There is nothing you trust more

You reveal everything to it

And it takes your secrets

Down to nowhere

Water is what you are missing

And even that someone you are missing

Is sixty percent water

What Do You See

What do you see
When you look
At me

You are a kind person
You would never look at me
The way I look at myself

I can't see myself from outside
I can look in the mirror
But still through my own
Distorted lenses

Not much to see
A messed up marionette
All tangled in strings
And broken
By illusion of freedom

What do you see
When you look
In the mirror

You are a humble person
You would never look at yourself
The way I look at you

I can't see through your eyes
I can see your eyes
But still through my own
Distorted lenses

It's a beautiful view
Two magical crystals
Where I try
To read the future

What do you see
When your eyes are closed

You are a smart person
You must be seeing beautiful things

I can't read your mind
I can just guess
But still through my own
Distorted lenses

I just wish I knew

I have bought a ticket

For a seat

In your personal darkness

Inspiration

Every time
I inspire somebody
I think

Am I worthy
To inspire

I am not
But the inspiration is

Crescendo

It starts again with soft and quiet sound
To say that everything is in the tune and set
And you are ready to be left to stray and found
But that's just start the best is not there yet

Shy whistle from a flute comes on to scene
It hears approaching busy steps of drum
New expectations for a story fills the screen
And questions rise of what is more to come

Then violins join in to see what happens
And cautious trumpets watches from the side
The road to beauty is so smooth and flattened
Conductor waves to switch from slide to slide

The choir of the sounds submerged in drama
And they are pulling you ahead in mighty train
Then thunder ends and peace of Dalai Lama
Is offered in droplets of the rain

The train slows down and stops before the station
What happens next is hidden from the scene
You maybe call it if you like abomination
But that is how composer made it be

So here you are in nowhere and it's raining
And lost is all direction and momentum
The tiers from skies are now already draining
It is your time to find your own crescendo

Decision

A moment can change eternity

Eternity can flash before your eyes

In a moment

Is there any difference

There are those moments

That takes you away

When you are not on your own

In your consciousness

And your mind

Swears submission

For eternity

For a moment

It will feel like it's for eternity

But you must decide

Between those two

It will take you a moment

Or eternity

Contamination

I'm looking at a white empty page
What is it telling to me
I can't work around this stage
When there is nothing to see

I try to look inside my self
Inside my mind and my heart
Even that doesn't work very well
Thoughts are hidden so far

Sorry no poem from me today
This feeling I always have hated
I am infected with emptiness
I am contaminated

My Bedroom Window

My bedroom window is a curious kid
Plays out and brings everything home
Every sound every smell from drainage lid
And it never leaves me alone

It barks like a dog when a stranger goes by
It waves its tail for delivery van
It longs and it waits and it waves goodbyes
It greets every moon every sun

At night it gets a bit calm and weary
It puts aside his people and cars
Stops playing and unfold the canvas
Starts quietly drawing the stars

Droplet of Salty Water

Whatever waves or swings
Like past or future ghost
There is always little droplet
Thrown out into the coast

Then landed on the grass
It shines like morning dew
It dries when day arise
Like all of them would do

Still living in the air
Translucent silky thread
It's free from all despair
Its soul I should've said

And then you breathe it in
But rather felt than seen
And take the drop within
Where it has always been

This droplet deep in mind
At times you know at night
It climbs over your eyelid
And falls but that's alright

Stick

I threw a stick into the fog

To see if someone throws it back

Somebody approached me

And asked

Why are you throwing sticks

From the fog

Tides

A tide stands up
Spreads its hood like a cobra
Attacks the coast
Then looses its balance
Falls down on its nose
And crawls back to the see

It stands up again
Raged by the storm
Triggered by its currents
Powered by the thrust

But the storm doesn't last
Soon little waves takes place
And calmly sizzling
In the orange evening sun
Under crystal blue skies
Slowly starts braking
The rock

Shapes of Love

There is a love
That has a shape of heart
A beating heart
And sometimes beating hard

There is a love
That has a shape of flower
It can have fruits
That sometimes can be sour

There is a love
That has a shape of bird
It has a song
That sometimes can't be heard

There is a love
That has a shape of present
But then again
There is no perfect event

There is a love
That's put away on shelf
No shape is not important
As much as love itself

Spring Theory

There is a theory
That winter is followed by a spring
That things
Are going to get better

And if they are not
It means
The bottom
Has not been reached

But as soon as that happens
A sudden improvement is expected
The sun will shine
Flowers bloom
And you will just jump
In the meadow
Poink poink poink

That Smile

It was so unique and so special
Your smile with a secret in it
Maybe assessing credentials
Trying if everything fits

With so much to find and to learn
To top up the credit of trust
We already know that this quest
Is laced with a droplet of lust

You always get me somehow mended
My day so much needed your print
And now almost unintended
I dropped you a subconscious hint

I don't know I think that you melted
I think that you picked up my touch
Your smile had a sound it was scented
My god I love you so much

Meaning

I worshipped you
In my dream
And now I wonder
What could that mean

People from the Future

I'm clearing the site for my future
Every brick of the old construction
Has a heavy story

Happy and unhappy
But the foundation can't afford
To keep them all

People from the future
Comes over to support me
To see how I'm doing

They listen to all those stories
And I tell them
In a great detail

They don't judge or complain
They just appreciate my work
I'm doing for them

I'm now exhausted
Have done enough for today
Will continue tomorrow

People from the future

Says goodbye and leaves

Thank you for coming

I'll see you next time

Parallel Universe

I'm sitting in a traffic jam
Looking for a wormhole
To get to the place
In time
Failing of course

There is no control
Time is racing itself
All you can do
Is to let time by
Bye time
I miss you already

This universe
Couldn't even start
Without a bang

There are people
Married more times
Than Saturn has rings

There are heroes
Gone through winds
Higher than ones
On Jupiter

Yet every effort
Every sacrifice
Small or big
Eventually ends up
In a black hole
Of simple
Everyday problems

Am I just another victim
Of a meaningless entropy

But then you smiled at me
I have now
Some evidence
Of a parallel universe

About the Author

Guntis Brazma is a poet who moved to England from Latvia in December 2009. Then as he started to get used to language he started to write poems in English too. *Tree Falling in Forest* is his first poetry collection.

guntis.brazma@gmail.com

Printed in Great Britain
by Amazon

79529453R00068